Luana Portales

I0119368

MI CASA es MI CASA

Wider Perspectives Publishing ¤ 2025 ¤ Hampton Roads, Va.

The poems, illustations and writings in this book are the creations and property of Luana Portales, the author is responsible for them as such. Wider Perspectives Publishing reserves 1st run rights to this material in this form, all rights revert to author upon delivery. Author reserves all rights thereafter: Do not reproduce without permission except Fair Use practices for approved promotion or educational purposes. Author may redistribute, whole or in part, at will, for example submission to anthologies or contests.

© 2025, Luana Portales, including writing as LU
1st run complete in April 2025 Wider Perspectives Publishing, Hampton Roads, Va.
ISBN 978-1-964531-00-7
2nd Gen ISBN 978-1-964531-06-9

Dedication

I dedicate this book to love.

The love I've shared, lost, found, forgotten

and will remember,

especially the one that gave me the courage

to write this book.

I also dedicate this book

to every being that is ready for change.

May you find peace in your journey,

and home within yourself.

Contents

Bored Games 1

Present! 3

Daddy Issues Snaps 4

Irony 6

Take Out 7

Lava' 9

The Dress 10

coLUmbuS PIZZArro 12

Working Out 17

Hanging Over 18

Mommy Break 19

Late to the Party 21

F-I_ne 22

Thirsty Friend 24

a masochist 25

When are YOU Coming Home 27

The Stay 28

Not About Christmas 30

No strangers in the house 31

Lu-VB-er 32

My Heart Was Racing Home 35

Same Meal, Different Plate 38

Loving Art 40

Hair Care After Flake Out 43

Old Friends 45

Jackpot! 47

Papi, Papi 49

RECEIvePt 53

HER MINE O' ME 54

Homesick	56
YOU're Welcome	57
House Play	58
Poet's Poem	60
Colores de Amor	62
B	63
I Struck Coffee to the Ground	64/66
Cranking Me Up-Side Down	68
Two Hearts, One Home	69
The Thing With a Dirty Fridge	70
Growing Pains	72
Pretty Little Birds	74
I'm done with pretty	76
I Run Target and Home Depot	78
I Fixed My Sink	80
My Aunt and Her Roommate	82
My Mamma Said	85
Strawberry Season	88
@be_lu_v	90

Bored Games

My family and I
used to play – house

House with a script
Lines in the walls

My parents
used to play – love
My brother
used to play —games

I played
—to be happy

We played
– for so long
It felt real

Doodles in my emotions
so deep

Miss—understood
Playing is not for children
It's for adults
Kids know
when the game
is over
But adults play – along
until everyone loses
I lost – myself
before I met me
in a game
in a house
in a family
Only finding
I've been playing – myself
All along

I learn love and games
and family belong to house
Family game night
Excuses— me
from home

Present!

My mom forgot the
       candles,
but he missed all of them.

He blew his chance
as I was blowing wishes.

      Miss opportunity
every year
      -ning
of me
blew up.

Daddy Issues Snaps

Mami chose daddy
Daddy didn't choose me
Christmas time reminds me
Of 2 daddies
        I used to write to Santa
              Please fill the void
With toys and food and attention
            I miss daddy
He's missed- too many Christmas to count
     on him
Santa always came thru with them toys
So I asked Santa to bring my dad back
Just to hear mom
To write my letter again
She doesn't believe in holiday spirit
     I guess
Kids know no better
She no longer believed   -in   -my dad
I wrote to Santa again
Put my letter under the tree
          I didn't mean to upset anybody
Santa is just a lovely man
In love with my mom
Santa became my dad
He tucked me in every night
     And I know
        I was his favorite elf
Favorite elf never made the toys
Quality Assurance
My department
I pick   -dad

Reassurance
Dad picks me up
And never let's me go
Christmas felt like
My birthday
Pointy big ears
Tiny little girl
I choose papi
          Papi always chooses me
Daddy issues   -love
To heal the absence
Papi issues presence
I believe in Santa
Papi believes in me
He's my favorite gift
Never quite made it
to the Christmas list
But fatherhood
      is not something you ask
Love issues papi
Daddy issues snaps

Luana Portales

Irony

I'm the villain
        everyone seems to love.
Help me even.

I'm burning the house,
        waiting for your cape
to appear.

I nurture fire
        and dance in flames.

I don't need salvation.
I crave your help,
        your chill,
        your attention.

And I terrorize as much,
        as many
        as I can.

Can't you see?
        I'm burning up
        from your hero complex.

Take Out

My mom served me thighs
        she don't like
And expect me to love them
Other kids jumped trampolines
While I jumped to low-rise
Insecurities
Show off   -the
Crack   - a laugh
Cracking up the fat kid
Hiding my legs
Like secrets
Y2K
More like
Y2thick, kid?
I was a 10
And always wanted to be a 0
Trendy to starve a kid
But mom fed me 5 times a day
I sound silly now
Like instagram and porn
Don't have a thick women category
Like BBLs are not the trendiest accessory
Like Kim K don't owe her assets
To Jlo
NOW
But I grew up
In thigh gaps
And the new diet will crack!
Dust drugs and get rid of
60 pounds in 2 weeks
I used to cry

And pray to G-O-D
For Bulimia!!!
Let me lose
     50 pounds or myself
Anything to fit-in
Like my thighs don't thunder
     when I walk
Like my stretch marks
     aren't lines that nature brushed
I eat, and serve, and cook
I loved the weight that left more
     than the weight that stayed
Found out that it was easier
     to love the weight
     than to drop it

Lava'

Her warmth poses as heat,
        but poisons like burns.

I've been cold for so long.
Her flames don't shape her demons,
        but the coat I've long for.

The scorch runs so deep
        that when she disappears,
it feels nice to aid,
                enough to heal
and nurture her next awakening.

We're a twin pack of icy hots,
                boiling ice cubes.
Not enough to drink,
                        just sipping.

Always thirsty for more.

The Dress

Obsessed with looking like a child,
like puberty never slapped her,
with itty bitty arms
and hips that never grew

                       -up

wide   -open to receive

                       -children

perfect soft skin,
no wrinkles, no acne
no scars that tell stories,
a girl,
no expression lines,
never looked up a thought in her life,
no frown lines,
erase all the stories,
the good and the bad ones,
looks like a child,
so small and tiny

                       -ready to be loved

tiny little waist,
she deserves to
eat a little, and
fit in

                       -the dress.

coLUmbuS PIZZArro

I coloniiiiiiiiizzed [English]
    and made it   my own
I tooK a language that is not *mía*
    and made it feelllllll like home.
I spl   it   word   s,
    impregnate(d) them
    & make them sound just like me.
Cris?   Columbus…
    Im biggeRR, badder, and better than him.
I par–t and <u>unite</u> oceans.
    I don't make you pick between
    the boat
    or
    the motion
I let English come
    and go
    as it wants to.
            She my lady, too.
I make my tongue RrroLL, too.
    Let me speak in Tongues for you.
I make English sound brownnnnn.
    My accent a threat
Pum,
    pum,
        pow.
My accent sickkk, mannnn.
    I'm worse than Pizarro.
        I'd do a killing.
    I slit throats and choke them,
        they just trying to say my Last name

Don't call me queen,
      call me *Reyna.*
I conQueered English,
      and I can speak how I want,
      right how I want.
They say I fucked English up,
            and I didddd.
I made her scream my name, and moan, too.
      Sorry you can't relate to.
They say I make her sound dirty, too.
      I'm not a founding father,
      but She calls me *papi.*
      I bet she don't do that for u.
I make English sound silly and funny, too.
      She a clown, *payaso.*
      She Breaks her own rules.
But I kill, kill, kill, kill.
I killed the verb to be
      b/c I am
           I was and will always be
           hispanic.
My accent ain't nothing, but
      a political act.
My accent so strong:
      It votes
      educates
      and liberates
      the stigma you got on me.
Maybe you don't know,
      but I pain   t,
I make the green-go
      cry and wail.
I painted my passport blue,
      but I got an accent,

so, that'S not enough for u.
She's not mine or yours.
      She a   hoe.
      She for the people.
      Because we the people.
      It's all of us
Specially if we chew and spit English,
      I want to hear accents so heavy,
      it breaks down discrimination.
           I want to hear accents so thick,
           it switches from bottom to top
           and turns on
                congress for better education.
      I want to hear accents so broad,
      it opens minds, drills Ignorance,
      and doesn't let it become racism.
No espiko inglés.
      Spanglish is my best
      ASSet.
People like me
      build English, too.
I find it revolutionary
      that everyone
      and their mamas
      claimed English to be their native tongue.
When English has never belonged to none
I'm sorry.
      I made English trip
               and fall for me.
English may starve
      if it wasn't for me.
I took English as land,
      Write the will to my kids for me.

Maybe I'm not a colonizer,
maybe my accent is a protest,
    & my pronunciation is reclaiming back
    what it is mine.
I just
    decolonize Englishh
    with my accent
I'm not spicy,
I talk with spice,
    and I defy,
because THIS tongue
    is a movement.
And I dreammmmmm
    that one dayyyyyyyy,
      English
      discovers
          freedom.

Working Out

I wish she'd pull me like her weights
Lift me up high, tight- no space
I wish she'd flex me like the scale
Heavy, strong -carry me home, light weight
I wish she'd take me like a scoop
Dry, like a shot, listened -never leave me on a loop
I wish she'd want me like a GYM
A lifestyle to be together thick or slim
I wish she love me like a protein shake
Shake me so hard just to drink of me like a lake
I wish she'd want me like her leggings
Every day, Hug her so tight. She's got my fingerprints
I wish she'd tell me we can work it out
Pull our own weight, kiss and say you're my partner Out Loud
I wish she'd stop aching of a Sore heart
I skipped the wrong day, it wasn't smart
I wish I'd told my mom I wasn't going to the gym
I was going to her -house and learning how to swim
I wish I wouldn't be drowning in my own lies
Keeping a straight face and queer eyes
I wish I came out at 16
I wouldn't be wishing she'd be with me... at the gym

Hanging Over

I knew the day was becoming bad
when we all skipped breakfast.
I am the lead of broken souls' house.
And I take care of the broken.

Mommy Break

This is not a break up letter.

I'm not here

    -to ask you
to be part of my life.

I don't believe in breaks
    -with love;
you break with love that doesn't nurture.

Mother is always right.

More like an independence letter

    -to the mother that may not nurture me
and breaks with love what nature brings.

I'm the nature that breaks

    -Mother with child

Child is not wombed to mother's nature

I can't break up with nature,
    but you can break with   love

Me

-a love that looks like me

You can teach me to be like

-mom,

But would you learn to love for me?
Would you love who I choose as much as me?

you'd exchange your last breath
for my first

Mom knows best,

even when it comes to her own life
But would you live for me?
Would you nurture your body once I leave
feed yourself love without greed
Would you stop   doing my favorite foods
and learn   to do your own?

Once I live,
Will you call our house a home?

Take care of yourself
and find the woman before the babies.

Late to the Party

Sour candy hugs,
Kisses covered in chocolate,
And smiles as mushy as marshmallows.

Muy dulce,
empalagoso, even,
to serve our sweet on a plate

Displayed on the table
I thought I was bringing
the cake,

But they whip me up
stir me up
and revamped me
as the pinata.

Let's celebrate
As I break down
While is not the kids
playing.

F-I _ne

"GIRLLL, YOU SO FIIIINE!!!!"
Echoes in the costume I've chosen
I have big red shoes to fill
Hilarious
How many meals have I skipped?
For some room-
to gaze at me
Suddenly my hair frizzes up
Only a hat would cover-
the silliness
the lack of nourishing
Teeth cleannnn
SMILE big and BITE
      -the hook
       -up
     -and down and up
      and downnn
Practice to not get caught
Laugh
It's your act
Pale face
sugar levels are down
No energy
Maybe I can try to throw up this time
Cough blood
It matches my nose
Pinocchio
Growing lying to yourself
rather than growing
      -up
and down

and up and down
like the scale
Bouncing in big pants
like balloons in the air
I'm not afraid of clowns
I've made one of myself
But it's okay
I'm fine

Thirsty Friend

I have gaslit myself
to convince my insecurities
we are friends
But friendship between us
it's quite the stretch

I ask for quality time
You shot o'clock
I want to life life
You want to pour me your way

I say I'm lost
You look at my hands
Reflection is the cure
my poison awaits

I can't stop swimming sober
I'm not behind the wheel
You choose control
cruising thru waters no one explores

This is not adios
breakdown the glass
Ice cubes
water down
your incapacity to empathize

I can smell your sinking
or am I just
to stay afloat
while I see you crash

a masochist

I want you to hit me- up
One more time
So we can fight with hands
What our lips can't
I'm sorry I pushed you -away
Like long distance wasn't enough
But unlike you I like it when it hurts
It makes us feel real
I don't know how to make love
I know only to fuck you up
I'm sorry
I'm too brusca
And now I beat myself up
Because I can't make you regret me
I can't torture you with the idea
That I am flawed
And that you shouldn't love me
I need you
To tell me I'm a good girl
I want you to hurt me so bad
I want to feel torn
I want to be mad- in love
Anything but the numb I carry
I want you to be you so bad
That I'm good
I want to be choked in apologies
Hug me so tight I stop breathing
Paint my pale skin with some color
Turn me red, purple and blue
I want be your favorite shade
Leave fingerprints on me

Like an art piece waiting on a blank canvas
Linger my blues
The quite and calm is torture
Show me different
Show me off
Love me so violently
That it feels kind
I'm sorry for overstepping
I guess I like it rough
Like stomping on my feelings
I miss to argue and get loud
I won't push you this time
I'll be soft
Like when we make up
our bruises

When are YOU Coming Home

My mind is so loud
I drive with no music
'When are you coming home?' echoes
On my mind like a cave with no end
I cave with no end
I crave fitting in
- a family that *awaits* my call
Rarely even calls
WHEN is part of the open question
That expects -me- to BE
I in Family
Even the cheapest option
Will leave me hungry
Is HOME even worthy?

The Stay

You fell in love with my suitcase
The way I pack
The art of keeping it together
and any other piece of our relationship that fit

I travel light
I'm ready- to go or to stay
To drop the keys at the door
My eyes asking you to take my suitcase-my baggage

We never learned to love
Or to be sorry
We only knew to pick on each other
Pick each other- up before we fall-too low

My insecurities- the ones you gave me
They start fights
you love the games
Where's the controller?

You push me- my buttons
My art destroyed
But it craves you for inspiration
Afraid of somebody to make you their muse

Butterflies- choke me
I mishandle I love yous
Insects overwhelm me
You ask me to stay

I was never the artist
Just the muse of your fights
I don't give you butterflies
Our promises are lies

between love and insects in your belly,
love stops suitcases
Feeds your belly
And makes you stay home

Luana Portales

Not About Christmas

Yesterday I told a boy
Santa Claus doesn't exist.
His face turned different colors
He longed for me to cave.
Change my sentence.
I didn't kill him.
He's allergic to peanuts,
not the truth.

no strangers in the house

Anxiety knocks on my door
    like a debt collector
Just to find
I'm not home
The car is outside
Knock knock again
    no Soliciting
I open the door every
    other time
Not today
    I do not owe you
        long talks
            about the future
I offer water
    make tea
Go at it again
Promising a better life
I am no longer interested,
    but I forgot she has an spare key
She takes care of me
    with worry
    overstays her welcome
Forgetting they come in pairs
Depression is quiet
    just waiting on her turn
    like I did not give up
    once they came in

Lu-VB-er

He was the one   -right?
I was the One   -driving home
he always Left me   -with his laaaaast word
my left hand
with his ring on
Drunk in love   -no
he holds the corona bottle
more than my hand

He let me drive   -on empty
I only drive   -him   -crazy
I maneuver the rocky roads of a failing marriage
My left hand Empty
because this is my laaast trip
he reminds me I'm tripping

And he Holds my hand
but not the way I wanted to
My way or the highway   -NO
but he holds on too Strong
I can't   -feel my fingers
My body is shaking
What have I done   -wrong this time?
I don't want to be right
he's just wrong   -for me

Keeeey
the car stoPS
he Pulled the *break*   -once again
he wants control   -of me
and my hand is Ssslipping

I'm done

I know he Punched   -the radio
but that Punch was meant for me
He likes to Hit me   -Up
with Punchlines
Only He thinks funny

He Chocked   -me   -hard
he Chocked all the *love* from my Heart
and the life Out of me
But he doesn't Hit women
He just likes to put them Down   -to sleep
And say I love you when no one's listening

I'm losing my hearing
or maybe the radio is as broken as me
I am sa-fe?
He's not abusing   -of me-right?
I'm abusing   -of him and alcohol
and I burn with rum
because burning our home   -be too much
I'm too much

He wants his ring baCK
like that wasn't my idea
I'm the One   -driving   -us -home
remember?

He Pulled me like a drink
and thank the universe
he always pulled Out
I'm about to Pull out   -home

It's sleepy time
We can   -sleep
dream   -for once
and tomorrow
we can handle the nightmare   -of divorce and disappointment
Sober of dreams together

Longest drive   -home
ETA 15 minutes
that's how long it takes to get married
but getting divorced
that's a longer   -poem.

My Heart Was Racing Home

My heart
                        was racing home.
I didn't belong
            to the pictures on these walls.
            I was gasping for air
like I have forgotten to breathe.

                        I walked on eggshells
Praying the sound doesn't wake you up.

Like the house,
I stayed still.

        My body   dropped cold,
I held onto tears.
I slipped and fell,
watering my belongings.

                    Our place was empty
Filled with crumbles of a house.

It not longer fit
            to get scratched by sharpened pieces.

I knocked your door,
your absence knocked me down one last time.

Goodbye decayed,
                with my willingness to stay friends.

I got outside,
                    before the rooftop kissed the floor.

I was   breaking   down
                                    to pieces,
to later know where it belonged.

        I drove   a box,
and unpacked my   home_work.

The tearing and breaking stopped.
The shattered bits glistened.
                        I was not broke   n

The new house was   under construction,
awaiting walls to be painted
my face.

The air was thinner

I danced   loudly for every breakfast,
nourishing nights with no medication,
falling only for me.

Carefree Barefoot walks   opened windows.
Memories visited a different reality.

You   were   a poem

        that I no longer enjoyed reading.

I home
        a puzzle that meant to break-down.

I would write you all over again.
Never regretting the pieces you kept of me.

My heart dashed   placement
and you gifted me a lovely nightmare.

I never left home
        I just gave her my name
now I play puzzles
            with other poems.

Same Meal, Different Plate

Your ex always cooked for you
and you loved to be fed.
You loved to not be hungry anymore,
even if they always forgot to season your food.
So you get attached,
and heartbreak deepens when they leave.
Nobody is taking care of you anymore.
You forgot you can cook for yourself.
So, you find yourself a new chef
with BETTER recipes.
And they leave because they hate *your* knives.
So, you stop eating.
But you gotta EAT!!!
So you find a restaurant,
and you eat from different chefs,
and no one cares if you liked their plate better.
There's always a new customer
and you're not ready to let go.
You don't want your belly to rumble.
You forgot to love yourself,
you were never ready to love.
If it was love,
you would be ready to let go.
Because you know the best meals
are the ones you make yourself.

So,
find yourself a cookbook
and try new recipes.
Maybe get new knives.
The kitchen is the heart of home.
You won't know what you like until you cook it yourself.

Loving Art

I make sculptures for the love I once had.
An almost empty gallery,
     maybe a small box worthy.

Love is an art piece that sells.
Exciting and fun before the commitment to work on it,
     but art pieces are *beauty* when they are dedicated time.
I'm definitely biased.

At the end, when the piece stays still, I study it.
That's the best part. I look and I see the flaws.
I daydream a different technique,
     a different brush, a different texture.
Just to walk away.

No one will notice what my eyes see.
Maybe someone else will love it and buy it.
Or maybe it breaks and it amps up the price.

People and overpriced love.
Overworking for something that was already broken.
Even shattered at times.

I mostly craft glass art pieces. People go crazy for those.
They love the form, the colors, how soft it looks.
Beauty on the outside and hollow inside.
Hollow glass holds enough space for overthinking.

Glass sculptures whenever they are finished, they are cold.
They look soft, but they're hard. Not strong, but brittle.
The colors of stained glass are just synthetic and toxic.

Mi Casa es Mi Casa

Glass transforms with the right heat. But also, glass breaks.
I pick up the pieces and heat it up again.
Although, when it shatters, I collect the sharpened dust.
Just to bleed my hands with unseen harm
        to create new sculptures with shattered glass as glitter.

I glued the red stained glitter because they glisten as my memories.
One day I will sculpt never ending art.
Hopefully I retire from glassblowing.
I will afford real glitter, not shattered second opportunity shimmer.

An art piece that may break and needs time,
        but that won't break me.
A love that will require a gallery.
The gallery of broken love stories and the one
        that I never shattered.
That's why I keep my box filled with art pieces.
No one else will make sculptures for the love I once had.

Hair Care After Flake Out

I was washing you
-out of my hair the other day
I felt dirty and my scalp wasn't itchy
My head felt so heavy
and I definitely needed a trim
Cut off the ex-cess
You convinced me
-that my hair always had to be shiny
You love my blowouts,
 when I straightened my hair
Priced me with heat
I no longer want damage
I like how my curls age
I love how frizzy it gets when it rains
The color has darkened with the years
But I'll love it even if pales and grays
I've cut it and start over millions of times
truth is I don't own a comb or hairbrush
But when you said you loved my hair,
I wish you meant fully
Untamed
Hiding my face
And running around the house
But like my hair and your fingers
I got tangled with the idea
They belonged together
But my head Is better -
off to be left alone

I should've never settled-
For a routine-
That was not meant for
The artistry
My shoulders were carrying

Old Friends

It should've read:
> "Anxiety knocks her door like a Jehová's Witness
> religiously, when least expected.
> Depression has root her down,
> like her favorite plants,
> by the window of her bedroom.
> So she stays still, but sees everyone moving."

It should've read:
> "Difficulty while breathing.
> Cannot perform her needs, and puts others' wants
>   on her chest.
> While depression holds her last breath,
> Anxiety is already thinking about robbing the next one.
> She can't breathe."

It should've read:
> "She sees potential and recruit's apologies within herself.
> Cannot Establish boundaries.
> Dreads direction and lacks movement from others, hers is
> no different.
> Get her to the finish line.
> She has no will to do it on her own."

It should've read:
> "Longs for a meal,
> but will starve for compassion.
> Drained by the thought of eating.
> She will hand spoon the needy
> and ignore the fact that food is one of her triggers."

Mi Casa es Mi Casa

It should've read:
> "She rode life too eagerly.
> She drove away from childhood,
> just to find out that growing up was a bigger
> disappointment.
> She has no drive and will crash at every bump."

It should've read:
> "She's lost
> or sick of trying.
> Seeking medical guidance.
> Hoping someone listens."

Instead, it read differently.
> "Trouble with adjusting.
> Signs of anxiety and depression."

No words would ever please her overthinking.
No diagnosis or treatment
could ever fill
the emptiness
she was feeling.

Jackpot!

Going
> home

as in

playing the slot machine

> slaughtering money and time
> > I do not have

Just to win win win win

> to drive or not drive
> to fly or catch a train

Gambling on emotions
that I cannot afford

> Losing
> control

Jackpot

> > Insufficient funds

My family is playing
> their favorite game

Let me try my luck
> one more time

> swipe

Always
    lighting up the casino

forgetting
    the house
        always wins

Papi, Papi

Papi I want to be a doctor
Papi I want to safe lives
Papi I want to make so much money
Papi all I want to do is be your pride

Papi I want to be a veterinarian
Papi I'd still be a doctor
Papi I want to work with dogs and cats
Papi I'll make tons of money and mom will never cry

Papi I want to be an artist
Papi I want to paint
Papi it's not about the money
Papi is all about sharing my pain

Papi it's not a hobby
Papi it's just me
Papi I'm an artist
Papi look at me

Papi papi

Papi I want to write
Papi I want to do more than read
Papi I love literature
Papi I'm just a lyricist

And this is our song

Papi don't worry about me
Papi I'll feed my soul with art
Papi I'll meet artist just like me
Papi my dream is to be seen

Papi I want to be an architect
Papi I want to go to a school in a different state
Papi I'll make so much money with my artistry
Papi I won't share my pain

Papi I can't afford school
Papi, can I come home soon?
Papi let me work with you
Papi I'll sell my soul

Papi papi

Papi imma live at sea
Papi look at me
Papi don't worry where I'll be
Papi this job ain't for me

Papi they make fun of my hair
Papi my accent, they don't understand
Papi I'm not flying planes
Papi I'm not the pilot, I only fix the engine bay

Papi some of them don't like my skin
Papi my food it's not it
Papi these people won't accept me
Papi I'm the only girl

Papi I hate this job
Papi I got 2 years left
Papi I don't belong at sea
Papi in two years idk where I'll be

Papi I'll be fine
Papi let me share my pain
Papi let me stay
Papi Virginia is all I am

Papi let me lose my mind
Papi nobody is kind
Papi I'll lose my pain
Papi I'll find my way

Papi I won't save the world
Papi let me share my thoughts
Papi I'll be kind
Papi I'll change your mind

Papi I'll find my own
Papi art will feed my soul
Papi art is not poverty
Papi art is the only time my mind is debt free

Papi this where I'll be
Papi catch me at the venue on thirty fifth
Papi I'll share my artsy pain
Papi look at me

Papi you may never apologize
Papi it's okay
Papi grandpa shattered your dreams
Papi you don't have to do the same

Papi this is my dream
Papi it's okay
Papi I love you
Papi look at me, we share the same pain

Papi you may never change your mind
Papi it's not too late
Papi I'll be fine
Papi follow your dreams because I will follow mine

RECEIvePT

I am the returned goods
from an online order,
waiting for someone   to get me.

Misplaced.
He asked me: "Where have I been?"
Like the aisles decided to part   ways,
so, he can walk to me.

Aisle one became two,
trying to shadow us
as an answer to his prayers.

Culminating the missed and found search.
He repeated: "Where have you been?"

An explanation
I never found words to.

We played scrabble
          one more time.
"Where have you been?"
Again and again.

He worries he's wasted time.
But I was here.
Misplaced.
Being the side character
of my own movie.
Watching life
from Home.

HER MINE O' ME

You'd say you'd love me raw.

Nobody, but me
loves that version.
She is too frail,
too sad, too mad.

She is not romanticized or sexy.
Funny hides from her.
Laughs swing on her mood.
If she was wine,
she wouldn't pair well with food.
Dry,
afraid of eating,
comfortable in her loneliness.

Do not approach if seen;
a package labeled handled with care,
but there's not a box she'd fit in.
She's all my rough edges
and every puzzle piece I haven't found.
Safe in between pages.
Bubble wrapped,
just so every word pops out her ears

Annoyed
Her heart is not like mine;
she lingers in the past
waiting to get hurt.

Alert,
seduced by jealousy
A poem that shouldn't be read out loud
I honestly hope,
You never meet her.

She might want to keep you
just so you learn to loathe her.

Mi Casa es Mi Casa

Homesick

I used to feel homesick
I felt displaced
Like my love never translated
My smiles looked heavy
Heavy grounded me
 never let me float out of reality
The outside was so hard to keep intact
Closed doors wasn't any better
I felt like a man
Unable to cry
Mi Papá taught me that
Crystallized by the culture shock
Ashamed that I felt numb
I don't remember how I got out of it
But I really thought I was done with that emotion
I preach that I am my own home now
But let me not see my bed for more than a night
I'll feel just like home was a placed I constructed by myself

YOU're Welcome

My house is like my heart,
not everyone is welcomed,
but if I let you in,
you would taste my love,
smell my essence
      and
           eventually,
                  go home.

House Play

I want to take you -home
Let you in
-My dirty laundry hanging
Let me -take you
To a warm cozy place you've never been
take off your
         -shoes please
I'm not cluttered
I keep the house straight
Unless
I feel lighthearted and carefree
You'll smell the burning candles
Warm up to
The low light
The mood set up to your liking
You're just a guest
But I'd love you to host
And take control-
As long as my boundaries are maintained
I like to take it slow
Lick the cup
-sugar rim
Make you sip-
Ginger tea and
         -feed you like a regular
Let you eat of-f
My plate
And once you're finished
I'll Hide the skeletons in the closet
I'll head for another load
Wash clothes and let them dry

Folding-
Because you gotta go
Do house things
Inside
I'm not good at playing
But if you're to stay
I got board games
Playing 2   - it's better
Because one   -got overplayed
And it's hard to open doors
Even worse to close them
It's taken a couple seasons
But I'm ready
I will get hurt and I will fall - deep
It's better if you stay over
And never go
But   -I can play house
All over again if I have to

Poet's Poem

he asked me for the love I write
She-e-e said you're the poet
Make a poem out of me
Write me bars so high,
I am never low of you
Don't leave me untitled
Call me yours
Let friendship sink
Sail the unknown
And let me navigate your overthinking
Say I make you heal
No fight or fly, now you talk and stay still
I uplift you like your favorite heels
Write about the space I give you
The peace of mind I give you
The pieces of me in you
Lose me in translation
Speak your love language
I want to hear your mother tongue
Roll your R's like your eyes
Dime Que me amas
Porque En español si te creo
Make sentences rhyme
You hate it when I call you my slime
You like Tequila on your lime
You bachata like a crime
Say I'm jealous of the good kind
You make me believe in the divine

And I've been waiting years to call you mine
So, I said fine
But you will be the poet
And I will be the love You write

Mi Casa es Mi Casa

Colores de Amor

I learned to love en Español.

Sometimes when you speak,
I get lost— in words I just learned.
You may be pouring — your soul.
Spotting — I missed you-r point completely.

All I hear is you-r love language.
I translate all tu amor para me,
but I miss all mine.
Mis palabritas y mi pequeña yo.

If you was to tell me
that little you learned to love in colores,
I'd paint you cuanto te amo.
Para que no te sientas azul.

No matter how much I pain-t,
you can't read me between lines.
Perdido como en-a-morado,
en colores que no necesitan translation

I don't need you to understand.
Solo dime que sí.
Y que algún día aprenderás
No por mí, pero por ti, carajo!

Porque mi amor habla en español
y ya me cansé de andar traduciendo.
Engañándote que creo en el *love.*
Cuando *amor* se escucha más fuerte.

B

Cheers to him

Who flies like a bird

Who is fly as ever

and like a feather

He will flow

I Struck Coffee to the Ground

I like my man like I like my coffee:
       Consistent.
With no spilled milk
Without regret I didn't ask for.
Keeping it 100% pure sugar.
Don't gimme the fake stuff.
Gimme all the calories.
Make my glucose levels crash.
Make me explode like candy crash.
Dulce De leche my coffee
Diabetes already in the family,
you the one missing.
be like my coffee: addicting
And not for everybody.
Love my mind and honor my body
then Let's make a blend.
I'll blend in all your flaws
I'll make your family my in-laws.
Grace me with your presence
       pour mistakes into lessons and drizzle them as blessings
Let me roast you like my coffee.
The steam will make you laugh.
offer a taste of you,
coffee with no milk.
Gulp me a love bigger than milk
A love so big
A love bigger than dick
Renown your last name as our brand
Let us multiply
franchise like Pit-bull: worldwide
We the kind of grounds worthwhile

Infuse me with your coffee eyes
I'll introduce love to brown eyes
reflection in a mug, honest eyes
And when Joe and Hazel want to play games
let's play coffee house
May I please get an American, at least 23 sugars
Actually coffee upsetting me lately
Instead I'll get a Chai and I'll replace the dairy for oatmilk
Matcha foam
I'm paying for my own drink anyway

Mi Casa es Mi Casa

Golpeé el Café al Suelo

A mi Me gustan los hombres como me gusta mi café:
Hecho a mi medida
Sin leche quemada
Sin arrepentimiento que no pedí.
Manteniéndo al 100% azúcar puro.
No me sirvas cosas falsas.
Dame todas las calorías.
Haz que mis niveles de glucosa salten al cielo
Hazme explotar como un caramelo.
Dulce De leche mi cafe
Diabetes ya esta en la familia, tú eres el que falta. sé como mi café:
adictivo Y no para todos.
Ama mi mente y honra mi cuerpo.
luego hagamos una mezcla.
Mezclaré todos tus defectos
Haré de tu familia mis suegros.
Dame gracia con tu presencia
vertire tus errores en lecciones y los rociare como bendiciones
Déjame tostarte como mi café.
El vapor te hará reír.
ofrece una muestra de ti, café sin leche
Ofréceme un amor más grande que la leche un amor tan grande
Un amor más grande que Nestlé
Reconoce tu apellido como nuestra marca. multipliquemos
Franquicias como Pit-bull:
para el mundo entero disfruta
Somos el tipo de terreno que vale la pena.
Infúndeme con tus ojos de café
Introducire al amor a los ojos marrones.
reflejo en una taza, ojos honestos
Y cuando Bailey's y a avellana quieran jugar

juguemos a la cafetería
¿Puedo por favor
conseguir un americano,
al menos 23 azúcares?
De hecho
el café me molesta últimamente.
En lugar de eso
compraré un Chai
y reemplazaré los lácteos por leche de avena.
espuma de matcha
Estoy pagando mi propia bebida de todos modos.

Cranking Me Up-Side Down

He kept the house at 69
Walked naked and
Only winter made him question
If he's walking too cold
Body bags warmed up
Better than his mind
Better than the baggage he carried
I carry new bags
But I don't put them down
Scared of being let down
I never asked to crank the heat up
      I'm cold
I was never meant to stay
69 doesn't cater to me
I warmed my- self up
Because you were too cool
To heat up
The idea
That I might not be the one
But I could be your only
It's too cold
      For me

Two Hearts, One Home

when i first moved in,
a dry clay awaited for my PAIN-t.
to BUTT-ER up my love for my house
i had to cure two hearts.

my ability to clout
always led ME to believe i needed fixing.
my kitchen like myself are
artwork that needed to be fettled to my liking.

my dishwasher let me break my favorite cUP.
pairing cleansing with more than dirTy dishes.
i no longer look for blame, but accOuntability
that PUZZLE together some rough edges.

i promised my kitchen that
i would stop paying for dishes i did not break.
but my cup like my energy,
i glued them up and gave them a new PURPOSE.

we were too old to come with instructions,
but my kitchen was older and she was doing just fine.
I'M SORRY if i break anything.
i tend to trip and fall when it comes to clay.

The Thing With a Dirty Fridge

It's that I could never
But I can't fathom to shame you or blame you
For vegetables that were neglected for too long
You had the initiative to choose organic
Not knowing that nourishment
Specially the boujie kind
Has a sooner expiration date
Somehow there's no berries
But sweet stains of what it once was
All kinds of plant milk collecting dust
But 2% running low
It tells me you had the best intentions of be someone you were not
But I don't need the evidence

Even though you've loved this cheese for what it looks like ever
You should let it go
It definitely has tasted better days
It's not your fault that they don't sell to singles
It seems like you either compromise to share
Or it goes to waste
The price of being unpaired
The really empty bottles are not really bad
They are also not worth the space
Sometimes it's okay to have an empty fridge
And start a list for groceries
Clearly there are things in this fridge
That are giving the ick
Again, nothing to hide your fridge for
I just can't expect to share a fridge with you
And ever expect for you to clean it
If you never had the desire to do it for yourself

Growing Pains

I'm emotional
A cry for help
Mom, I'm sorry
For not being grateful of you enough
And your presence
I am cramping and
you're not here   -to make me tea
I can take care of me
But I don't want to
I want you- and your soup
You made it look so easy
So flawlessly perfect living
And I'm struggling to get up and eat
Daughter gets upset with food mother cooked
And gets up saying mother could do better
Mother always does her best
Especially for her- (period)
Daughter should've done better
 it was your weekend too, mom
And you were preparing me for the week -and life -was a break
with you
And now life only breaks me down
I dreamt of being alone
And now I am -in so much pain
Me duele que no estés
Why is my belly so upset with me?
Or is my pancita upset
because you're not here
I'm so cold
And my body aches of womanhood
My mom never complained

I don't see me get up and cooking for two kids
With this pain
I only have to take care of the baby
And I'm failing
Everyone has to stop upsetting the baby
My body doesn't know of another baby
But myself
Carrying the weight of being a woman
The baby needs her mom
The baby struggles with adulthood
And needs a plan B
Plan A didn't work out as always
Thank the universe for the beginning of my cycle
The journey of being empathetic with mom
We sync-chronize our love
My body counts soup and tea
Dinner is sleep and hunger
a spoonful of Tylenol
Because LU-ber Eats is not working
And mom is coming over tomorrow
To fix me- a plate

Pretty Little Birds

Pretty little birds ♫ Pretty little birds ♫ Pretty little birds

♫ Mami Mami can't you see
What metal island is done to me ♫

I used used love my life
They call it metal island.
But island it was not
Hard and cold like metal
It attracted little pretty birds
They take your feathers
And give you metal wings
Convincing you can fly
But your Feet earthbound and connected
Metal island is nothing
but floating rust
Metal island is nothing
if you not in it
Their fetish
Little pretty birds
Metal island is like prison
Crime committed: you sign up for it
Their mission: to ensure the sea is blue
Filled up with tears of pretty little birds
Birds would go to freedom island
But it is cheaper to go to prison
And metal island
gives you a sense of freedom

The food is pretty much the same
And so is the energy
No one, not even the older birds want to do their time
And we all wait to put our metal wings to rest

♪♪ Mami Mami can't you see
I'm a bird that cannot fly
One day one day I'll be free

Leaving metal island behind ♪♪

I'm done with pretty

I'm done with perfect
Glass skin and glossy hair
I'm done with skin tight clothes
And gaspin for air
I'm done with pretty
-thick hair as long as i don't have to wax
Be ready to
Love all the dimples on all cheeks
All the cellulite paired perfect with my jeans
I'm done with other meats hanging around
But if it's about chicks
They gotta work it out
I'm done with pretty
I'm done with meeting English with a smile and nods like I don't
understand
I'm done with being understanding and being misunderstood
I'm done with acting and faking
And aching
I'm not an abused child
Just pretty enough to look like puberty never hit
Hit me with the expectations of being a woman
Hit me with the thigh gap and BBLs
Hit me with lactation size boobs and postpartum
Hit me with size matters if its my body
Hit me in a sexy way and not because you're mad
Because I'm done with pretty
And all the time it takes
All the safety measurements it breaks
I'm done with mirrors, tapes and scales
I'm done with fear
Walking fast to my car keys between my fingers

Mini skirts and crop tops apparently mean yes to sex
I'm done with hugs that lead to body bags
With drugs that don't belong in non-consensual drinks
I'm done with sorrys and worries
I'm done with father fucking pretty
Call me pretty when I'm in pain and I cry
Call me pretty when I pay for rent or my momma's car
Call me pretty when I wear loose clothes and you cant see my smile
Call me pretty when you ft me walking me to my car
Call me pretty when I don't want to go out with you or get some drinks with Carl
Call me pretty when I mess up my words or I don't get the punch line
Call me pretty when the only number I care about is my mother fucking credit score
Call me pretty when I'm safe
Call me pretty while I'm still alive
Call me pretty with all my ugly and disguise

I Run Target and Home Depot

I've lost 22 pounds since we broke up
My mom says I've let go of the happy weight
because I'm sad
She says heartbreaks can make you lose weight
I can put my feet down now
after being let down so many times
But I think it's because I changed my cardio
Now I go on target runs
And I target everything to my cart
Because you're not here to target me and make me stop
I am a runner
I run fast because I'm not good at walking away
I run with no direction, except away
I run with intention of not running in to you ever again
I am not into you, never again
 I'm trying to build myself
and build myself a kitchen
The heart of a home
Feed myself the love I've been craving
Trying to fix the cracks of my foundation with therapy
I go on Home Depot runs very often
and patching holes on the wall with this Gorilla drywall repair
I'm Lu the builder
Building self love and avoiding
Home Depot at 7
Now I go at 11,
To stop looking at all the good looking men trying to help me
sir I'm not lost,
I'm finding me

And if I was lost,
It be in you
 so I gotta run
And make it home soon
To the love of my life

I Fixed My Sink

May you buy a house
and never break

    down
Because it needs constant fixing
I was in *my place*
the kitchen
Washing off
DIRT

I am single
    both mom and dad to my house
So
 when I pulled out
    the faucet
And it broke
    water spitting on my face
      I cried
for my kiiiddd
BECAUSE I JUST PAID
for a new KITCHEN
    Mind you
I am NEW
to this mom thang
There's 2 babies crying
    I'm unsupervised
WHO WILL CALL THE PLUMBER????
Fix my sink
THIS IS MY
    house

I cry to the phone
after being mansplained
that my faucet needed
a tight hand
I slapped that BITCH UP
She is   fine   NOW
My kitchen
My faucet
My sink

My Aunt and Her Roommate

I wake Up to
      sunny Up-side
            down smiles
We share breakfast,
          books, and a kitchen
We got: Two
      kitties,
      three ferrets,
      and one BIG tiny HERmit crab
I don't ask Her to
          lower
          her voice,
     or her spirit.
And She doesn't mind that I love loud
      or like snacks,
        I disappear

The insurance people, and others that
      I shall not mention
      believe that we're lovers
And may Chloe be the closest thing
      I have to a happy marriage,
      I do not blame them

She carries my light
      and my heavy
      Cream

me in tea and honey
If she was any more sweet,
      like my mom,
      I'd be diabetic

Oh! Chloe has ruined me forever!
      I thought my standards high
      But she Jumped the Sky
                and fly

She is hope, presence, and faith combined
      My every prayer answered
      and the kind of Love
      you may Only feel once

I sadly am not   in love with Chloe Henry,
      she is straight, and
      my love
      has never reached that kind of bliss
      But blessed
      with someone's future breakfast,
      partner,
      I have been
So, to the love of her life,
      I'm sorry
      I'm borrowing your wife
      and unconvince everyone
      she's more than my sister

Mi Casa es Mi Casa

But may you Reach this kind of High
     I got Her
     until you find Her
She is hiding in my spare room
     next to my love and all my secrets

She is my every laugh,
     so I plead
     You take your time

My Mamma Said

I'm Latina
that my food always got spice
But my name is not spicy
Or dirty
Or difficult
My name like my hips
Shall twist and turn
Like music on your tongue
My mamma said I'm Latina
And we all don't look the same
So I don't have to burn my skin
Or straighten my hair
Latinos like their food
They're not the same
Yes a taco is tortilla and meat
And Gordita is a tortilla beans and meat
And yes it does sound like a burrito
And yes you can eat ceviche o mangu on taco Tuesday
And yes everything tastes delicious
And yes they are made by the same hands
And yes they are still different
My momma said I'm Latina
And Latinos are known for traditions
It's been passed from abuelita to abuelita
Like love
Like recipes
Like wealth
Like opportunity
Like oppression
Like food insecurity
Like being erased from history

Like underrepresentation
Like job insecurity
Like not being paid fairly for speaking español
Like dressing super fly on Christmas Eve
Noche buena asking santa for more coquito y pisco
My momma said I'm Latina
And family comes first
So only I
can tell my brother to go away
By the way he looks
His family is here
And Latinos like empanadas in between your teeth we stick
together
Yes I was born in Peru
And yes I love my country
And yes I'm immigrant
And yes I love Virginia
But please stop if you're not offering to pay for my ticket,
don't tell me to go back
You play with my feelings
Like nicotine in the lungs
It is not cancerous
But it makes a bad habit repetitive
Enough to kill the dreams inside
be careful with chain smoking
And the smokescreen intentions
Against the families looking for change
My momma said I'm Latina
And I should wear my Peruvian flag proud
I should never be scared of being loud
And I chose this country as my home
And if I can learn English
Like cooking tamales because it is nice to know and share,

but it's okay if you don't want to
If I can learn to pay my taxes
Like dancing salsa with the IRS
If I can respect the rights, beliefs and opinions of others
Please respect mine too
Because my momma said I'm Latina
And I love every part of me
I love my cultura mi música mi comida mi español y mis latinos
And my momma said if it's not nice, we don't get it

Strawberries' Season

We are on Peak
        of strawberry season
and my
     grandma Taught me about strawberries.

        And If you wanT the sweetest of sTRawberries,
you gotta go for the strawberries that been ready to be picked
        Up for a couple days now.
It is the Time and space,
     those couple extra days
     that makes strawberries have a sweet taste.

     Kinda... like me.
Except I do not neeeeeeed a couple of days,
     and I do not wish to be picked Up or fixeD.
I just need a couple of minutes and some   space
     And to pay you back,
I'll give you my sweet.
     Because space and time is what I need.
And I'll be as gooooooood as a sTRawberry.

     My kisses would taste just as
         red, sweet and fruity.
     My love would be as
        kind and patient.

But the unmistakable way that sTRawberries
     get pickeD   before Peak.
I've been around people that genuinely made me feel
     there was something wrong
        with me.

You see, nobody wants a strawberry that is not sweet.
You see, nobody wants a person on their low days, like me.
        And you understand that   because
You've been around people   that made you feel
                    like a rotten strawberry.

Been left alone for to long,
      starting to smell like compost.
Everyone eating   the better strawberries.
And we are just waiting to be left   spoiled.

But my grandma taught me about strawberries.
           The ones that no one picked,
      were always meant for something sweeter.

Like her love and strawberry jam.

@be_lu_v

Let it be love,
because pain called
     and you answered
     just in time

It was time to build
     and you fell

        in love

Painting walls
     rather than building them

      Designing doors
      to open for yourself

Let it be forgiveness,

          not forgotten

Open the mail
and pay your dues

Ignoring the box
     doesn't mean
     you don't have to
     check it

Let it be healing,
       even if the key
doesn't fit

Let home
     be at peace

Mi Casa es Mi Casa

Luana Portales

Acknowledgements

When one writes poetry, one must know that it will be costly. I wrote this book to seek peace and redifine what ached me. My first step was awareness, which is the space I wrote in. Emotions and trauma are hard to navigate, but the work is highly favored when you lead from a place of love. I believe poetry is healing, but it was not the last step in my journey. Please seek help. Call 9-8-8 if you're experiencing a crisis.

This book of poetry was written on the clock, somewhere in the Mediterranean Sea, my house, and somewhere between open mics. Monday nights at the Venue on 35th have completely ruined me! I have grown spoiled by the amount of talent I have experienced. The worst part is these individuals are extremely inspiring. Beware of the amount of prompts and love they will send your way.

Now my flowers:

I'd love to say thank you to everyone who's shared their presence with me. I am so very thankful of my editor! TEECH! You're the best! Shout out to the Venue on 35th! Jorge, James, and Shanadiah! An special thanks to the Performers' Playground, Writers Rec Room, and every space that builds love for the arts! Love you and thank you to my Verb Benders family *past, present and future*, you have completely spoiled me and my little legs! An extra thank you to Ari and T Rex, my unconditional lovers. Thank you to my family and friends! Thank you to my mom and dad for

letting me be, even if I be too much of my being! Thank you to my Self-Love Book Club girlies *you've changed my life*! The idea of publishing was gifted from Symay and Daniel, thank you for your encouragement. I love you all! Thank youuuuuu <3 Thank you to every space I've shared with love! Thank you to my motherland and to the state I call my home. Dear reader, you're also loved! And thank you to me, for loving me even when it was hard. Thank you for trusting me to build us a home.
Finally, thank you to my love. May you grow fonder and even more spoiled!

With much love,
Lu <3

Colophon

Wider Perspectives Publishing regrets to have to announce that the ongoing Colophon page, used to tout artists published in books from WPP, has to be reworked. This is due to the growing library of fine writers coming out of, or even into, the Hampton Roads area of Virginia.

Samantha Casey
Donna Burnett-Robinson
Faith Griffin
Se'Mon-Michelle Rosser
Lisa M. Kendrick
Cassandra IsFree
Nich (Nicholis Williams)
Samantha Geovjian Clarke
Natalie Morison-Uzzle
Gus Woodward II
Patsy Bickerstaff
Edith Blake
Jack Cassada
Dezz
Daniel Garwood
Jada Hollingsworth
Tabetha Moon House
Travis Hailes- Virgo, thePoet
Nick Marickovich
Grey Hues
Rivers Raye
Madeline Garcia
Chichi Iwuorie
Symay Rhodes
Tanya Cunningham
     (Scientific Eve)
Terra Leigh
Raymond M. Simmons
Samantha Borders-Shoemaker

Taz Weysweete'
Ann Shalaski
Jade Leonard
Darean Polk
Bobby K. (The Poor Man's Poet)
J. Scott Wilson (Teech!)
Charles Wilson
Gloria Darlene Mann
Neil Spirtas
Jorge Mendez & JT Williams
Sarah Eileen Williams
Stephanie Diana (Noftz)
Shanya – Lady S.
Jason Brown (Drk Mtr)
Kailyn Rae Sasso
Crickyt J. Expression

Crystal Nolen
Catherine TL Hodges
Kent Knowlton
Maria April C.

the Hampton Roads
     Artistic Collective (757
     Perspectives) &
The Poet's Domain
are all WPP literary journals in
cooperation with Scientific Eve or
Live Wire Press

Check for those artists on FaceBook, Instagram, the Virginia Poetry Online channel on YouTube, and other social media.

www.ingramcontent.com/pod-product-compliance
Lightning Source LLC
Chambersburg PA
CBHW031440270326
41930CB00007B/793